Copyright © 2023, Melissa C. Dyer. No content may be reproduced with out the expressed written consent of the Author.

Unless otherwise noted, all Scripture quotations are taken from the Holman Christian Stand Bible®, Copyright © 1999, 2000, 2002, 2003, 2009 by Holman Bible Publishers. Used by permission. Holman Christian Standard Bible®, Holman CSB®, and HCSB®, are federally registered trademarks of Holman Bible Publishers.

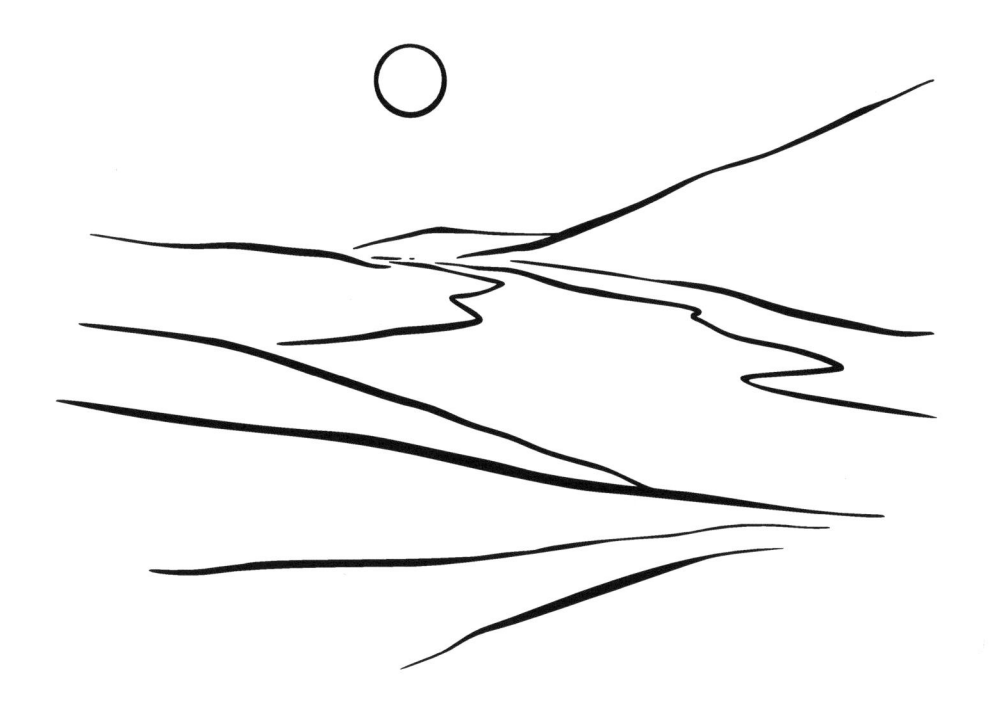

Contrary to everything you may have learned or heard about the Christian life, it is all about receiving. This is the essence of grace. And the means by which we grow in our relationship with God. We open our minds, hearts, and souls to receive salvation, healing, and restoration. Every action we take is a response to grace. This 40 Day Guided Journal is a tool, only a tool, for you to use as you seek to respond to the grace awaiting you. Think of it as an aide to receiving what God wants to give you. I believe He wants to infuse you with holy strength. He wants to infuse you with courage.

Every step of faith you take into the expansive life God has for you will require courage.

Noah, Moses, Elijah, and Jesus, what do they have in common? A forty day and forty night journey requiring courage. What was it like to be on the ark? Other than the noise and smell from all those animals, what was it like to experience rain for the first time and witness with your own eyes the people and land swept into liquid oblivion? When would it stop? When would it be safe again? The waiting. The fear.

And our friend Moses shrouded in a cloud of thunder hearing from God. Forty days and forty nights taking it all in, writing it on the stone tablets. Overshadowed in God's mighty power, unprotected and alone. Elijah, after fleeing for fear of death, made the forty day and forty night trek to the mountain to hear from God. Confronted with a storm before receiving the still small voice of instruction. Each of them, Noah, Moses, and Elijah experienced what it is to draw courage from the wilderness.

How well would you do to be held in a forty day and forty night season of vulnerability?

Exposed to the elements and totally reliant on God, would you be afraid? How patient would you be to the process of listening for God's revelation to you? These are the challenging questions we face in our wilderness seasons. This is how we cultivate courage from the wilderness. The wilderness is a place meant to make you, not break you. Let's take a forty day journey together and discover how to cultivate courage from the wilderness seasons in our life as we learn from Jesus' example.

For the next forty days we'll observe the work God wants to do in us in seasons of wilderness. We'll also look closely at Jesus' testing in the wilderness and pull out the Biblical applications we can apply to our lives to gain courage and holy strength for the tests coming our way. Be encouraged, a wilderness season can prepare you for breakthroughs and blessings on your spiritual journey. Use these forty days and forty nights to draw closer to God as an act of wholehearted devotion to Him, God has spiritual power He wants to give you. Let's learn to embrace the wilderness as the place and space we give ourselves over to God for His glory and our good. Thanks for joining me.

May the Lord Bless You and Keep You Beloved,

Melissa

1

We'll begin our journey into the wilderness by reading the account of Jesus' testing in this place where we confront fear and temptation. As we begin to direct our attention to this key passage of scripture there are several significant details we should notice. The first being this account appears in three of the four Gospels; Matthew, Mark, and Luke. Reading all three of the accounts will aid us in our understanding. I've provided them here for you in a single translation. I recommend you also read these passages in two more translations, of your own choosing, as well.

Here is the account of Jesus' temptation or "test" in the wilderness as translated from the Holman Christian Standard Bible.

Matthew 4:1-10

1 Then Jesus was led up by the Spirit into the wilderness to be tempted by the Devil. 2 After He had fasted 40 days and 40 nights, He was hungry. 3 Then the tempter approached Him and said, "If You are the Son of God, tell these stones to become bread."

4 But He answered, "It is written:

Man must not live on bread alone
but on every word that comes
from the mouth of God."

5 Then the Devil took Him to the holy city, had Him stand on the pinnacle of the temple, 6 and said to Him, "If You are the Son of God, throw Yourself down. For it is written:

He will give His angels orders concerning you,
and they will support you with their hands
so that you will not strike
your foot against a stone."

7 Jesus told him, "It is also written: Do not test the Lord your God."

8 Again, the Devil took Him to a very high mountain and showed Him all the kingdoms of the world and their splendor. 9 And he said to Him, "I will give You all these things if You will fall down and worship me."

10 Then Jesus told him, "Go away, Satan! For it is written:

Worship the Lord your God,
and serve only Him."

Mark 1:12-13

12 Immediately the Spirit drove Him into the wilderness. 13 He was in the wilderness 40 days, being tempted by Satan. He was with the wild animals, and the angels began to serve Him.

Luke 4:1-13

1 Then Jesus returned from the Jordan, full of the Holy Spirit, and was led by the Spirit in the wilderness 2 for 40 days to be tempted by the Devil. He ate nothing during those days, and when they were over, He was hungry. 3 The Devil said to Him, "If You are the Son of God, tell this stone to become bread."

4 But Jesus answered him, "It is written: Man must not live on bread alone."

5 So he took Him up and showed Him all the kingdoms of the world in a moment of time. 6 The Devil said to Him, "I will give You their splendor and all this authority, because it has been given over to me, and I can give it to anyone I want. 7 If You, then, will worship me, all will be Yours."

8 And Jesus answered him, "It is written:

Worship the Lord your God,
and serve Him only."

9 So he took Him to Jerusalem, had Him stand on the pinnacle of the temple, and said to Him, "If You are the Son of God, throw Yourself down from here. 10 For it is written:

He will give His angels orders concerning you,
to protect you, 11 and
they will support you with their hands,
so that you will not strike
your foot against a stone."

12 And Jesus answered him, "It is said: Do not test the Lord your God."

13 After the Devil had finished every temptation, he departed from Him for a time.

Imagine being confronted directly by the Devil. Fear embodied with an agenda to engage in a direct assault. Have you ever had to face evil head on? I truly admire anyone who can run straight into danger, especially physical danger. Maybe this is why I thoroughly enjoy watching action adventure movies. I find the ability to engage in conflict inspiring. Sometimes I even imagine what it would be like to endure fierce physical training in preparation for a fight. Equipping myself to prevail in combat. Gravitating to the physical is a natural response when confronted with fear and evil. We either fight or flee. But the Jesus way shows us a different path.

The first detail I noticed when reading these passages above is the weapon Jesus used to fight, His was a spiritual weapon, not a physical one. Maybe you're familiar with what the Apostle Paul referred to as, God's armor. In Ephesians Chapter 6 (verses 10-18) we are instructed to put on the whole armor of God and to stand firm when we are tested. We are encouraged to pick up the sword of the Spirit, which is the word of God, as our weapon. And this is the very way Jesus fought His battle with the Devil. He used the sword of the Spirit, the word of God. But not just God's word, but specifically verses from the book of Deuteronomy. We'll learn more about the significance of this as we journey together.

The second detail I noticed when reading these passages was the length of time mentioned, 40 days and nights. Whenever we see specific numbers like 7, 12, and 40 in the Bible our spiritual senses need to perk up. We need to pay attention.

There are some quantities which have importance to God and even if we don't know why they need to become important to us. God desires to reveal Himself to us and wants us to see His established patterns and rhythms as our Creator. Life may seem crazy and chaotic, but there is a steady heartbeat holding it all together. We need to learn to recognize that heartbeat so we can align our lives to its rhythm.

Here are a few examples of where we see these God patterns in scripture. There were 7 days of creation, 7 days of marching and the walls of Jericho fell, and 7 days of celebrating the Feast of Tabernacles. If we were doing a study on all the 7's in the Bible we'd notice this represents a pattern of completion to God.

Another numeric pattern found in scripture is the number 12. There were 12 tribes of Israel and 12 disciples, and the New Jerusalem will have 12 gates. So, we can glean a dozen holds some significance to God. It's not just the way we count off our eggs!

And there are many, many, 40's found in the scriptures. In the opening I referenced Noah, Elijah, and Moses. If we observe closely each of them experienced 40 days and nights of something. Noah was confined to the ark during the 40 days and nights of rain. Elijah traveled 40 days and nights to reach Mount Horeb. And Moses camped on a mountain with God for 40 days and night. Regardless, if our wilderness causes us to get wet, grow travel weary, or glory in God's presence in solitude, it's all a form of wilderness. And it's all significant to God. But, before we move into our study from Jesus' 40 days and 40 nights, let's revisit one more famous 40, or infamous should I say, from the Bible. The 40 years.

Let's set the stage. God's people were stalled in a wilderness for 40 years. What can I say, they failed the test, and as a result they missed the blessing. How did they fail? Fear. Fear overshadowed their courage. They just wouldn't take the steps of faith necessary to see God's strength in their weakness. Which reminds me how important it is to fight fear the way Jesus fought. The battle with fear is spiritual. And, I don't know about you, but I don't want to be stalled in the wilderness. Stuck in fear. Instead I want to follow the pattern Jesus used to pass the test and win the battle. Let's journey back in time to learn where the Israelites lost the battle, so we don't have to make the same mistakes. Then we can learn the Jesus way.

Jesus will show us the way in the wilderness to win the war with fear.

This is what we will be studying and applying for 40 days and how we will learn to cultivate courage from the wilderness, instead of getting stalled in our war with fear. God's on our side. He wants us to win. Drawing us into the wilderness is His way of getting us battle ready. He's got a plan and purpose for our testing.

There's a third detail I noticed, and I hope you did as well, when reading the account of Jesus' testing in the wilderness. God drew Jesus there by His Spirit. And guest what, He also drew the Israelites into the wilderness too. He had the same purpose for this season of wilderness time for both the Israelites and Jesus. It was to spend a period of time in privacy bonding with them to allow their newly affirmed identities to take shape. We can see a pre-wilderness pattern underscore this principle. Just before Jesus was drawn into the wilderness by the Holy Spirit He had been baptized. And at His baptism God affirmed His identity as the "Son in whom God the Father was well pleased." (Matt. 3:17) Similarly, the Israelites were drawn into the wilderness, led by Moses God's instrument, just after they had been labeled by God as His people. (Ex. 5:1) God wanted both Jesus and the Israelites to receive their new identities in Him.

Jesus was labeled by the crowd as the son of Joseph the carpenter and He needed to be proved as God's Son before He could fulfill the ministry God was calling Him to. The Israelites were labeled as captive slaves by the Egyptians, and needed to be proved as God's chosen people before they could inherit the promised land and be ambassadors of God to the polytheist and pagan peoples around them. The wilderness served as a place with space to release one's old identity, one's past and receive a new identity for the future. As believers in Jesus Christ we all need to spend time in the wilderness for this same purpose.

We need to be drawn away to a spacious place to bond with God as His son or daughter and as a member of His chosen people, a member of His family of faith. And as we follow Jesus' journey in the wilderness we can learn how to prove ourselves as a child of God. We can learn to combat fear with holy courage that leads to spiritual power as He did.

Jesus will show us the way through the wilderness to win the war with fear.

There are three battles we'll learn to win as we journey with Jesus;
- The battle of putting God first.
- The battle of trusting God and having faith.
- The battle of worshiping God alone.

What would it look like in your life to put God first, trust Him and have faith, and worship Him alone for 40 days? Are you willing to cultivate courage as you commit to "wilderness" time with God to increase your spiritual strength? This is the journey we'll be taking together. How exciting to imagine the results of such a commitment.

After Jesus endured His time of testing in the wilderness He was released to minister to the unbelieving and broken world around Him. A world in desperate need of His spiritual strength. Without it, salvations, healings, and miracles wouldn't have been possible. Jesus was just like us in His need to power up with God. He had to lay down the essence of Himself which could not be contained within the confines of a human body, mind, and soul. He laid the super part of Himself aside to participate in the natural. He shared our same limitations. The mental, emotional, and physical. However, within those limitations was able to fast and pray for forty days and nights. We know this because the scriptures confirmed His limitations as it says, "He was hungry." (Matt. 4:2)

The question we're holding is, how do we emerge from the wilderness with courage like Jesus instead of getting stuck in fear like the Israelites? And this will require we look at both encounters. There is a proverbial fork on the wilderness road and we're going to learn how to spot it so we don't go astray.

To begin let's look back at how the Israelites responded in the wilderness to;
- The battle of putting God first.
- The battle of trusting God and having faith.
- The battle of worshiping God alone.

In Exodus Chapter 16 we're shown how the Israelites reacted to their hunger in the wilderness. It's a good reminder Jesus faced this very same test. Let's read how the Israelites responded.

> Exodus 16: 1-5
> 16 The entire Israelite community departed from Elim and came to the Wilderness of Sin, which is between Elim and Sinai, on the fifteenth day of the second month after they had left the land of Egypt. 2 The entire Israelite community grumbled against Moses and Aaron in the wilderness. 3 The Israelites said to them, "If only we had died by the Lord's hand in the land of Egypt, when we sat by pots of meat and ate all the bread we wanted. Instead, you brought us into this wilderness to make this whole assembly die of hunger!"

> 4 Then the Lord said to Moses, "I am going to rain bread from heaven for you. The people are to go out each day and gather enough for that day. This way I will test them to see whether or not they will follow My instructions. 5 On the sixth day, when they prepare what they bring in, it will be twice as much as they gather on other days."

Did you notice how they reacted when they got hungry? In verse 2 it says they "grumbled." Other translations use the word, complained. In our house sometimes we use the word hangry. HUNGRY + ANGRY = HANGRY. When my daughter was a tween (almost teenager) she had a favorite t-shirt she wore, on a too regular basis. The imprint on it read, "I'm sorry for what I said when I was hangry." We learned this wasn't just relatable to our family. Passersby would stop us and ask where we'd purchased it! It was a missed opportunity for a profitable side hustle I suppose because we humans get very grumbly when we get hungry. Spiritually though we need to identify our hunger as a test. Let's look at God's response to this group of hangry people in the wilderness.

Look at verse 4, God says He will "test" them to see if they will follow His instructions. Do you see the test. He was setting them up to be obedient not to be disobedient. God's setting His people up to prove themselves by their character. Will they put Him first and obey, or will they compromise to satisfy their hungry bellies?

Jesus on the other hand, when tested by the Devil to doubt God's care and provision for Him withstood the temptation to satisfy His momentary discomfort. Instead He responded in faith and used what God had already provided for Him as evidence of God's provision, His word.

We can choose to react or to respond. We can be defensive or offensive. It's simply a matter of achieving a tactical advantage in the battle. The Israelites had no idea God could make it rain bread! God was about to show them another way He could deliver them out of an impossible situation. Wasn't that worth the hunger?

Moving on, let's take a look at battle number two. How did the Israelites react when God invited them to trust Him and have faith?

Numbers 13

1 The Lord spoke to Moses: 2 "Send men to scout out the land of Canaan I am giving to the Israelites. Send one man who is a leader among them from each of their ancestral tribes." 3 Moses sent them from the Wilderness of Paran at the Lord's command.

And at the end of their 40 day journey, surprise surprise another 40 day learning opportunity, what did they report when they returned? It says;

25 At the end of 40 days they returned from scouting out the land.

26 The men went back to Moses, Aaron, and the entire Israelite community in the Wilderness of Paran at Kadesh. They brought back a report for them and the whole community, and they showed them the fruit of the land. 27 They reported to Moses: "We went into the land where you sent us. Indeed it is flowing with milk and honey, and here is some of its fruit. 28 However, the people living in the land are strong, and the cities are large and fortified. We also saw the descendants of Anak there. 29 The Amalekites are living in the land of the Negev; the Hittites, Jebusites, and Amorites live in the hill country; and the Canaanites live by the sea and along the Jordan."

30 Then Caleb quieted the people in the presence of Moses and said, "We must go up and take possession of the land because we can certainly conquer it!"

31 But the men who had gone up with him responded, "We can't go up against the people because they are stronger than we are!" 32 So they gave a negative report to the Israelites about the land they had scouted: "The land we passed through to explore is one that devours its inhabitants, and all the people we saw in it are men of great size. 33 We even saw the Nephilim there—the descendants of Anak come from the Nephilim! To ourselves we seemed like grasshoppers, and we must have seemed the same to them."

You see that? The scouts, the leaders saw how good this land was with their own eyes. This land God was promising to His people. They also brought back evidence to show the people. For 40 days, both the leaders and the community were given the chance to trust God and have faith that He would do as He said He would. They were given a time to prepare to receive His blessing. In verse 2 God says clearly He is giving the land to the Israelites, but instead of trusting God and having faith they allowed doubt and fear to take over.

Jesus, on the other hand, when faced with the test of putting His safety on the line, like the Israelites were facing, responded with trust and faith. Let's look again at Matthew 4:5-7

> 5 Then the Devil took Him to the holy city, had Him stand on the pinnacle of the temple, 6 and said to Him, "If You are the Son of God, throw Yourself down. For it is written:
>
> He will give His angels orders concerning you,
> and they will support you with their hands
> so that you will not strike
> your foot against a stone."
>
> 7 Jesus told him, "It is also written: Do not test the Lord your God."

This is the paradox with trust and faith in God. The goal is to fear the consequences of disobeying God, not of facing our enemies! Jesus knew God the Father was the ultimate source of all strength and power and a healthy fear of Him wielding that power is for our good. And just as the Israelites and Jesus were surrounded by cultures who oppose God and His ways, so too are we. It's an everything goes way of thinking, that is unless we choose to obey God, then we experience opposition. You'll know which side you're on and which battle you're facing when you can answer the question; Which choice requires holy courage and spiritual strength?

Are you seeing the pattern here? The struggle between seeing the natural battle before us and using the supernatural to win it. These are the perfect intersections to ask the question, WWJD? What would Jesus do?

This phrase originally made popular by a well read book of the early 1900's, In His Steps: What would Jesus do? Addressed the very same questions we're asking here on our journey with Jesus. But, you probably recognize the acronym from it's 1990's resurgence on wristbands, one of which my tween daughter also wore, most likely, while wearing her hangry t-shirt. How appropriate!

Now before we leave our fearful companions, the Israelites in the desert of their destruction, let's revisit the epic tragedy of their failure to worship God alone during their wilderness training. We'll read while Moses was on the mountain receiving God's laws for worship, for 40 days and 40 nights, the people grew impatient, took matters into their own hands, and pursued man made gods. Exodus 32 says this;

> When the people saw that Moses delayed in coming down from the mountain, they gathered around Aaron and said to him, "Come, make us a god who will go before us because this Moses, the man who brought us up from the land of Egypt—we don't know what has happened to him!"

Really. They couldn't sustain 40 days and 40 nights of waiting? I don't think, if you're reading this, you will melt your jewelry down and make an idol to worship, but how often are we tempted to take matters into your own hands instead of waiting on God? We're all tempted to use other tactics to win our battles instead of choosing to be patient for God to show us the way. Which is exactly what Jesus chose to do when He was tempted to shorten His seasons of waiting. The Devil tempted Him to exit His immediate pain with a shortcut to glory. The account in Matthew says;

> 8 Again, the Devil took Him to a very high mountain and showed Him all the kingdoms of the world and their splendor. 9 And he said to Him, "I will give You all these things if You will fall down and worship me."
>
> 10 Then Jesus told him, "Go away, Satan! For it is written:
>
> Worship the Lord your God,
> and serve only Him."

Jesus will rule over all the kingdoms of the world. And He's earned this privilege through His death on the cross. Jesus had the chance to skip His suffering and compromise, but He didn't and nor should we. God is creating beautiful purpose from our suffering and we only get to see it when we choose to worship Him alone and wait for Him to reveal it to us.

Now, after all those failings of the Israelites, some of which we may personally identify with - let's be honest, we may find ourselves discouraged by the battles we've lost in our past.. But, we can't let this discouragement set in and keep us from future growth. Even if we're questioning how we can be confident of our ability to be like Jesus, surrendering again and again will train us to cultivate our courage and strengthening us in the process.

Here's what I've learned on my own spiritual journey. The more I give myself over to God, surrendering to the power of the Holy Spirit, the more I will live as Jesus did with holy courage and spiritual strength. And, Jesus shows us under the covenant of grace, the new covenant of His blood, being re-born of the Holy Spirit, we are able to be tested and tried in the wilderness and emerge with courage. Even if we've failed before. Getting stalled isn't an inevitability, it's only a sign we're battling fear. If we take a step and then another and another our courage will be strengthened and we can, like Jesus, experience a spiritual breakthrough.

It is possible to prove our identity as sons and daughters of God. We don't have to be like the first generation of Israelites (the ones who languished in the wilderness) who let fear rob them of God's blessing. Who we identify with is our choice. We can decide.

Chapter's 11 and 30 in the book of Deuteronomy clearly demonstrate the power of our choices. We can choose to obey God and be blessed. Or, we can disregard God's instruction and suffer the consequences. Let's read both of these chapters together to gain understanding of the strategy God gives us in the wilderness to prepare us for spiritual victory.

Deuteronomy Chapter 11

1 "Therefore, love the Lord your God and always keep His mandate and His statutes, ordinances, and commands.

2 You must understand today that it is not your children who experienced or saw the discipline of the Lord your God: His greatness, strong hand, and outstretched arm; 3 His signs and the works He did in Egypt to Pharaoh king of Egypt and all his land; 4 what He did to Egypt's army, its horses and chariots, when He made the waters of the Red Sea flow over them as they pursued you, and He destroyed them completely; 5 what He did to you in the wilderness until you reached this place; 6 and what He did to Dathan and Abiram, the sons of Eliab the Reubenite, when in the middle of the whole Israelite camp the earth opened its mouth and swallowed them, their households, their tents, and every living thing with them.

7 Your own eyes have seen every great work the Lord has done.

8 "Keep every command I am giving you today, so that you may have the strength to cross into and possess the land you are to inherit, 9 and so that you may live long in the land the Lord swore to your fathers to give them and their descendants, a land flowing with milk and honey. 10 For the land you are entering to possess is not like the land of Egypt, from which you have come, where you sowed your seed and irrigated by hand as in a vegetable garden. 11 But the land you are entering to possess is a land of mountains and valleys, watered by rain from the sky. 12 It is a land the Lord your God cares for. He is always watching over it from the beginning to the end of the year.

13 "If you carefully obey my commands I am giving you today, to love the Lord your God and worship Him with all your heart and all your soul, 14 I will provide rain for your land in the proper time, the autumn and spring rains, and you will harvest your grain, new wine, and oil. 15 I will provide grass in your fields for your livestock. You will eat and be satisfied. 16 Be careful that you are not enticed to turn aside, worship, and bow down to other gods. 17 Then the Lord's anger will burn against you. He will close the sky, and there will be no rain; the land will not yield its produce, and you will perish quickly from the good land the Lord is giving you.

18 "Imprint these words of mine on your hearts and minds, bind them as a sign on your hands, and let them be a symbol on your foreheads. 19 Teach them to your children, talking about them when you sit in your house and when you walk along the road, when you lie down and when you get up. 20 Write them on the doorposts of your house and on your gates, 21 so that as long as the heavens are above the earth, your days and those of your children may be many in the land the Lord swore to give your fathers. 22 For if you carefully observe every one of these commands I am giving you to follow—to love the Lord your God, walk in all His ways, and remain faithful to Him— 23 the Lord will drive out all these nations before you, and you will drive out nations greater and stronger than you are. 24 Every place the sole of your foot treads will be yours. Your territory will extend from the wilderness to Lebanon and from the Euphrates River to the Mediterranean Sea. 25 No one will be able to stand against you; the Lord your God will put fear and dread of you in all the land where you set foot, as He has promised you.

And moving on to Chapter 30 we read;

Deuteronomy 30
30 "When all these things happen to you—the blessings and curses I have set before you—and you come to your senses while you are in all the nations where the Lord your God has driven you, 2 and you and your children return to the Lord your God and obey Him with all your heart and all your soul by doing everything I am giving you today, 3 then He will restore your fortunes, have compassion on you, and gather you again from all the peoples where the Lord your God has scattered you. 4 Even if your exiles are at the ends of the earth, He will gather you and bring you back from there. 5 The Lord your God will bring you into the land your fathers possessed, and you will take possession of it. He will cause you to prosper and multiply you more than He did your fathers.

6 The Lord your God will circumcise your heart and the hearts of your descendants, and you will love Him with all your heart and all your soul so that you will live. 7 The Lord your God will put all these curses on your enemies who hate and persecute you. 8 Then you will again obey Him and follow all His commands I am giving you today. 9 The Lord your God will make you prosper abundantly in all the work of your hands with children, the offspring of your livestock, and your land's produce. Indeed, the Lord will again delight in your prosperity, as He delighted in that of your fathers, 10 when you obey the Lord your God by keeping His commands and statutes that are written in this book of the law and return to Him with all your heart and all your soul.

11 "This command that I give you today is certainly not too difficult or beyond your reach. 12 It is not in heaven so that you have to ask, 'Who will go up to heaven, get it for us, and proclaim it to us so that we may follow it?' 13 And it is not across the sea so that you have to ask, 'Who will cross the sea, get it for us, and proclaim it to us so that we may follow it?' 14 But the message is very near you, in your mouth and in your heart, so that you may follow it. 15 See, today I have set before you life and prosperity, death and adversity. 16 For I am commanding you today to love the Lord your God, to walk in His ways, and to keep His commands, statutes, and ordinances, so that you may live and multiply, and the Lord your God may bless you in the land you are entering to possess. 17 But if your heart turns away and you do not listen and you are led astray to bow down to other gods and worship them, 18 I tell you today that you will certainly perish and will not live long in the land you are entering to possess across the Jordan. 19 I call heaven and earth as witnesses against you today that I have set before you life and death, blessing and curse. Choose life so that you and your descendants may live, 20 love the Lord your God, obey Him, and remain faithful to Him. For He is your life, and He will prolong your life in the land the Lord swore to give to your fathers Abraham, Isaac, and Jacob."

The whole book of Deuteronomy is a restating of God's faithfulness to His people and the commands He had given them to live as people of faith. It's no wonder Jesus used verses from Deuteronomy to combat all three tests of the Devil He endured in the wilderness. He was putting God's command into action.

Faith in and faithfulness to God is proof of our relationship with Him. Jesus shows us how He used Deuteronomy 11:8 to win each battle. He modeled scripture memory as a powerful weapon we use in times of spiritual testing. The Holy Spirit will remind us of what God says, THE TRUTH, in times when the Deceiver (another name given to the Devil, or as Jesus called him, the Father of Lies) wants to lead us away from winning these key three battles;

- The battle of putting God first.
- The battle of trusting in God and having faith.
- The battle of worshiping God alone.

Therefore, as part of our 40 Day journey together we will commit 8 key scriptures to memory. They are;

Deuteronomy 4:7
7 For what great nation is there that has a god near to it as the Lord our God is to us whenever we call to Him?

Deuteronomy 6:5
5 Love the Lord your God with all your heart, with all your soul, and with all your strength.

Deuteronomy 6:6-9
6 These words that I am giving you today are to be in your heart. 7 Repeat them to your children. Talk about them when you sit in your house and when you walk along the road, when you lie down and when you get up. 8 Bind them as a sign on your hand and let them be a symbol on your forehead. 9 Write them on the doorposts of your house and on your gates.

Deuteronomy 8:17-18

17 You may say to yourself, 'My power and my own ability have gained this wealth for me,' 18 but remember that the Lord your God gives you the power to gain wealth, in order to confirm His covenant He swore to your fathers, as it is today.

Deuteronomy 10:12

12 "And now, Israel, what does the Lord your God ask of you except to fear the Lord your God by walking in all His ways, to love Him, and to worship the Lord your God with all your heart and all your soul?

Deuteronomy 29:29

29 The hidden things belong to the Lord our God, but the revealed things belong to us and our children forever, so that we may follow all the words of this law.

Deuteronomy 30:15-16

15 See, today I have set before you life and prosperity, death and adversity. 16 For I am commanding you today to love the Lord your God, to walk in His ways, and to keep His commands, statutes, and ordinances, so that you may live and multiply, and the Lord your God may bless you in the land you are entering to possess.

Deuteronomy 32:3-4

3 For I will proclaim Yahweh's name.
Declare the greatness of our God!
4 The Rock—His work is perfect;
all His ways are entirely just.
A faithful God, without prejudice,
He is righteous and true.

Jesus also shows us how this act of obedience to Deuteronomy 11:18 is evidence of His equipping us to prevail in our moments of testing. Let's look at Chapter 30 vs. 11-14 again;

> 11 "This command that I give you today is certainly not too difficult or beyond your reach. 12 It is not in heaven so that you have to ask, 'Who will go up to heaven, get it for us, and proclaim it to us so that we may follow it?' 13 And it is not across the sea so that you have to ask, 'Who will cross the sea, get it for us, and proclaim it to us so that we may follow it?' 14 But the message is very near you, in your mouth and in your heart, so that you may follow it.

When we hide God's word in our hearts it's within our reach. It becomes near to us, on the tips of our tongues. Ready for us to respond to the tests and temptations that the Devil uses to entrap us with, causing us to lose faith and become discouraged. This is how Jesus prevailed in the desert. And this is how we can too! We'll be using a five fold method of scripture memory I call READ, WRITE, SAY, SING, MOVE. You don't have to complete all five steps at the same time, however, you won't have to complete all five steps in the same sitting. But completing all five steps daily is important. You can also use index cards if more convenient for you.

- Step One : READ - read the verse slowly.
- Step Two : WRITE - write the verse out.
- Step Three : SAY - say the verse aloud.
- Step Four : SING - sing the verse to a familiar melody. (ex. Mary had a little lamb)
- Step Five : MOVE - this can be done one of two ways, you can create motions with your body matched to phrases in the verse (similar to a choreographed dance) or you can write the verse on objects (I've used seashells for this) and move the phrases around fitting them in order. The goal here is to use kinesthesis as a memory tool.

Therefore, let's commit to these 40 days of drawing courage from the wilderness by challenging ourselves to train up for;

- The battle to put God first.
- The battle to trust God and have faith.
- The battle to worship God alone.

This is an intentional season of honest reflection, journaling, prayer and hiding God's word in our hearts. I'm confident that we will emerge with more courage and spiritual power to face the testing and temptations in our future because of it. Remember, this dedication, using this Guided Journal as a tool, sets us up to receive the holy strength God wants to impart to us. This committed time is a response to His grace.

Here's how we'll get started on this journey together. On the following pages you will find 40 days worth of journaling for prayer and to respond to the daily reflection questions. You will also be committing one of the eight verses to memory for every five day period. This way you can use this as a resource to accompany you for 40 consecutive days or for an eight week period, five days a week. Maybe a Monday to Friday commitment fits best in your schedule. Whichever you choose the outcome will yield spiritual strength, this I'm sure of!

AND

Since we're taking this journey together I'd love to hear from you. I'm always blessed to receive emails or messages through social media sharing all the ways God is working in your life so please do share. My email is Melissa@MelissaCDyer.com and you can tag me or send me a message through Instagram at @MelissaCDyer_

Now let's begin.

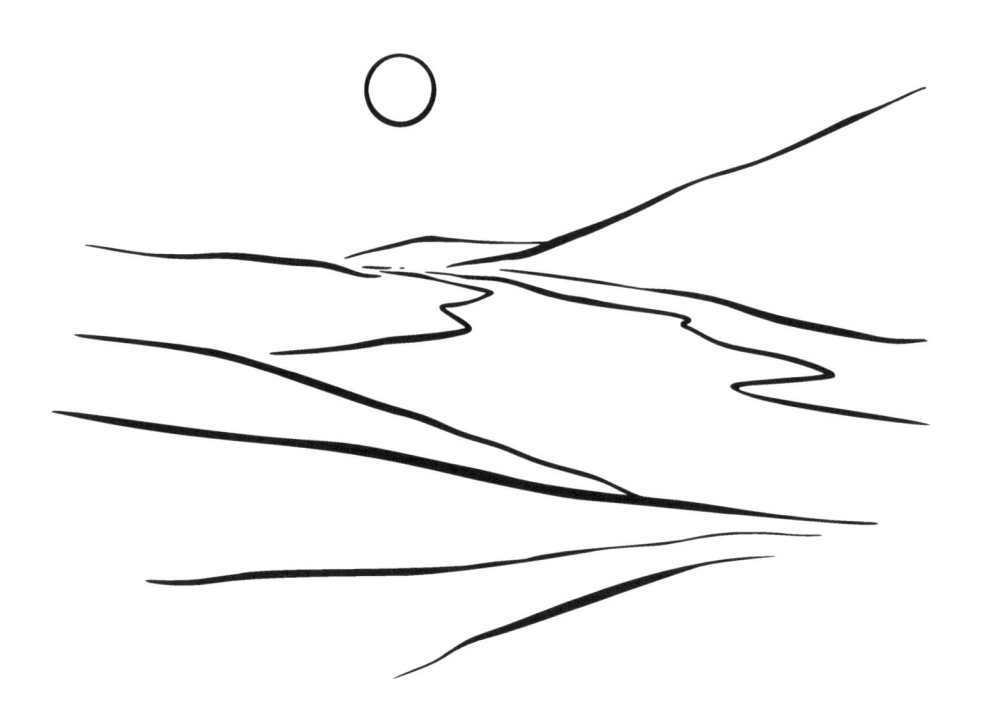

Verse One

DEUTERONOMY 4:7

FOR WHAT GREAT NATION IS THERE THAT HAS A GOD NEAR TO IT AS THE LORD OUR GOD IS TO US WHENEVER WE CALL TO HIM?

5 Minute Journaling

WHAT AM I BATTLING TO PUT GOD FIRST?

_____
_____
_____
_____
_____

WHERE AM I BATTLING TO TRUST GOD AND HAVE FAITH?

_____
_____
_____
_____
_____

HOW AM I BATTLING TO WORSHIP GOD ALONE?

_____
_____
_____
_____
_____

Prayer & Meditation

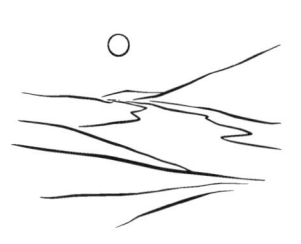

PRAY FOR GOD TO HELP YOU WIN THESE BATTLES.

_____
_____
_____
_____
_____
_____
_____
_____

READ, WRITE, SAY, SING, AND MOVE TO THIS DAY'S VERSE.

_____
_____
_____
_____
_____
_____
_____

5 Minute Journaling

WHAT AM I BATTLING TO PUT GOD FIRST?

_____
_____
_____
_____
_____

WHERE AM I BATTLING TO TRUST GOD AND HAVE FAITH?

_____
_____
_____
_____
_____

HOW AM I BATTLING TO WORSHIP GOD ALONE?

_____
_____
_____
_____
_____

Prayer & Meditation

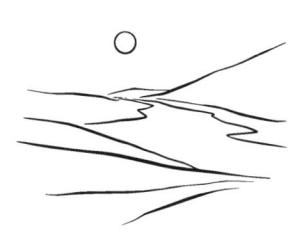

PRAY FOR GOD TO HELP YOU WIN THESE BATTLES.

_____
_____
_____
_____
_____
_____
_____
_____

READ, WRITE, SAY, SING, AND MOVE TO THIS DAY'S VERSE

_____
_____
_____
_____
_____
_____

5 Minute Journaling

WHAT AM I BATTLING TO PUT GOD FIRST?

WHERE AM I BATTLING TO TRUST GOD AND HAVE FAITH?

HOW AM I BATTLING TO WORSHIP GOD ALONE?

Prayer & Meditation

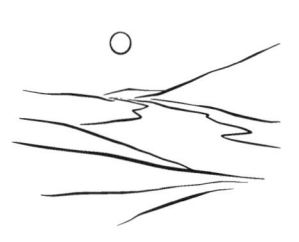

PRAY FOR GOD TO HELP YOU WIN THESE BATTLES.

_____
_____
_____
_____
_____
_____
_____
_____
_____

READ, WRITE, SAY, SING, AND MOVE TO THIS DAY'S VERSE

_____
_____
_____
_____
_____
_____
_____

5 Minute Journaling

WHAT AM I BATTLING TO PUT GOD FIRST?

WHERE AM I BATTLING TO TRUST GOD AND HAVE FAITH?

HOW AM I BATTLING TO WORSHIP GOD ALONE?

Prayer & Meditation

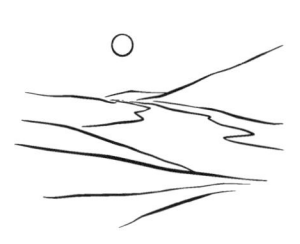

PRAY FOR GOD TO HELP YOU WIN THESE BATTLES.

_____
_____
_____
_____
_____
_____
_____

READ, WRITE, SAY, SING, AND MOVE TO THIS DAY'S VERSE

_____
_____
_____
_____
_____
_____
_____

5 Minute Journaling

WHAT AM I BATTLING TO PUT GOD FIRST?

WHERE AM I BATTLING TO TRUST GOD AND HAVE FAITH?

HOW AM I BATTLING TO WORSHIP GOD ALONE?

Prayer & Meditation

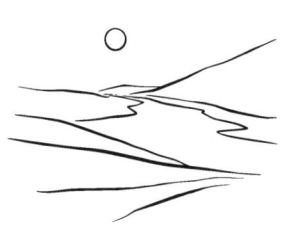

PRAY FOR GOD TO HELP YOU WIN THESE BATTLES.

_____
_____
_____
_____
_____
_____
_____
_____
_____

READ, WRITE, SAY, SING, AND MOVE TO THIS DAY'S VERSE

_____
_____
_____
_____
_____
_____
_____
_____

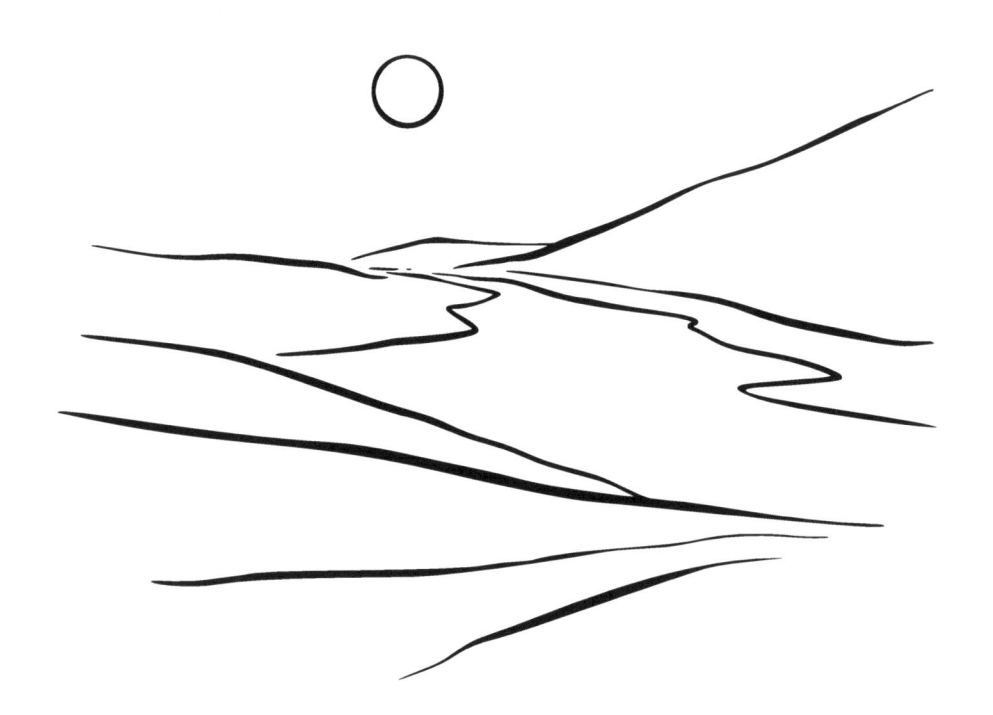

Verse Two

DEUTERONOMY 6:5

LOVE THE LORD YOUR GOD WITH ALL YOUR HEART, WITH ALL YOUR SOUL, AND WITH ALL YOUR STRENGTH.

5 Minute Journaling

WHAT AM I BATTLING TO PUT GOD FIRST?

WHERE AM I BATTLING TO TRUST GOD AND HAVE FAITH?

HOW AM I BATTLING TO WORSHIP GOD ALONE?

Prayer & Meditation

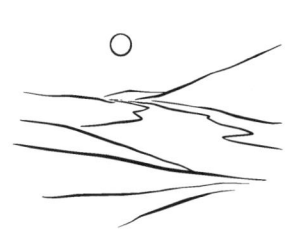

PRAY FOR GOD TO HELP YOU WIN THESE BATTLES.

_____
_____
_____
_____
_____
_____
_____
_____

READ, WRITE, SAY, SING, AND MOVE TO THIS DAY'S VERSE

_____
_____
_____
_____
_____
_____
_____

5 Minute Journaling

WHAT AM I BATTLING TO PUT GOD FIRST?

_____
_____
_____
_____
_____

WHERE AM I BATTLING TO TRUST GOD AND HAVE FAITH?

_____
_____
_____
_____
_____

HOW AM I BATTLING TO WORSHIP GOD ALONE?

_____
_____
_____
_____
_____

Prayer & Meditation

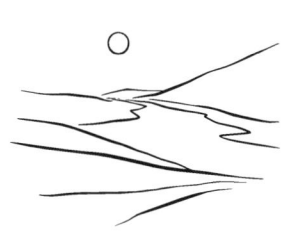

PRAY FOR GOD TO HELP YOU WIN THESE BATTLES.

_____
_____
_____
_____
_____
_____
_____
_____
_____

READ, WRITE, SAY, SING, AND MOVE TO THIS DAY'S VERSE

_____
_____
_____
_____
_____
_____
_____
_____

5 Minute Journaling

WHAT AM I BATTLING TO PUT GOD FIRST?

WHERE AM I BATTLING TO TRUST GOD AND HAVE FAITH?

HOW AM I BATTLING TO WORSHIP GOD ALONE?

Prayer & Meditation

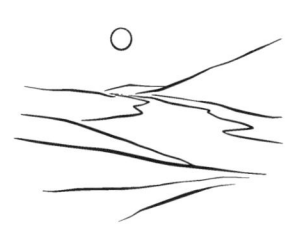

PRAY FOR GOD TO HELP YOU WIN THESE BATTLES.

_____
_____
_____
_____
_____
_____
_____
_____

READ, WRITE, SAY, SING, AND MOVE TO THIS DAY'S VERSE

_____
_____
_____
_____
_____
_____
_____

5 Minute Journaling

WHAT AM I BATTLING TO PUT GOD FIRST?

WHERE AM I BATTLING TO TRUST GOD AND HAVE FAITH?

HOW AM I BATTLING TO WORSHIP GOD ALONE?

Prayer & Meditation

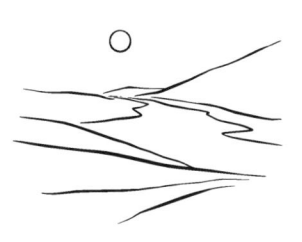

PRAY FOR GOD TO HELP YOU WIN THESE BATTLES.

READ, WRITE, SAY, SING, AND MOVE TO THIS DAY'S VERSE

5 Minute Journaling

WHAT AM I BATTLING TO PUT GOD FIRST?

_____
_____
_____
_____
_____

WHERE AM I BATTLING TO TRUST GOD AND HAVE FAITH?

_____
_____
_____
_____
_____

HOW AM I BATTLING TO WORSHIP GOD ALONE?

_____
_____
_____
_____
_____

Prayer & Meditation

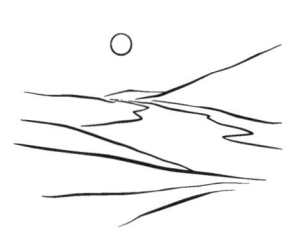

PRAY FOR GOD TO HELP YOU WIN THESE BATTLES.

_____
_____
_____
_____
_____
_____
_____
_____

READ, WRITE, SAY, SING, AND MOVE TO THIS DAY'S VERSE

_____
_____
_____
_____
_____
_____
_____

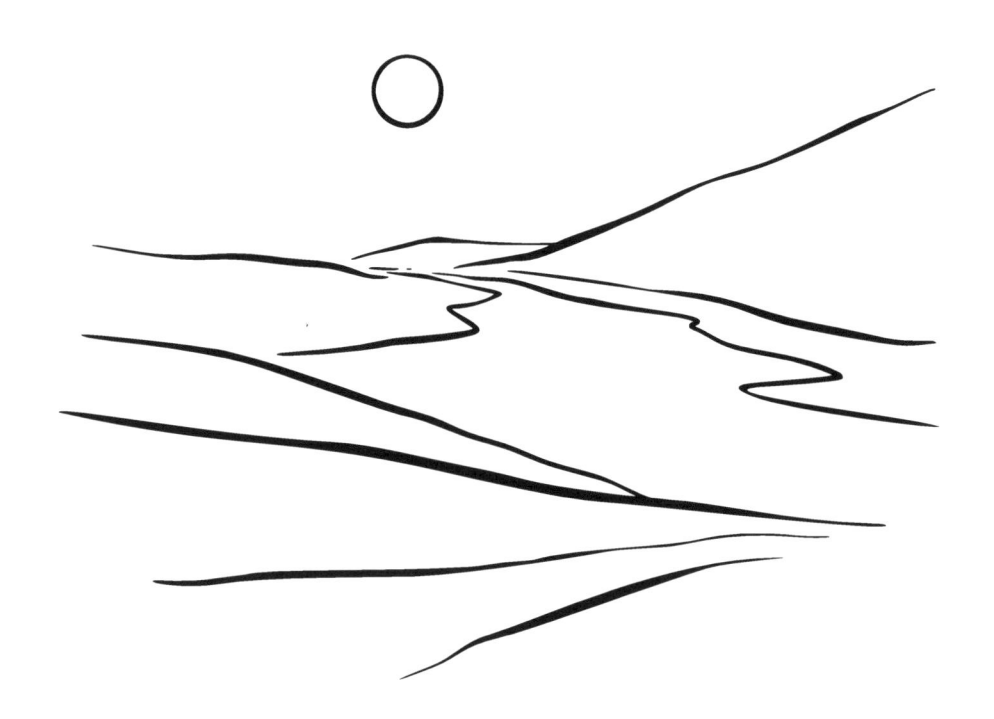

Verse Three

DEUTERONOMY 6:6-9

THESE WORDS THAT I AM GIVING YOU TODAY ARE TO BE IN YOUR HEART. REPEAT THEM TO YOUR CHILDREN. TALK ABOUT THEM WHEN YOU SIT IN YOUR HOUSE AND WHEN YOU WALK ALONG THE ROAD, WHEN YOU LIE DOWN AND WHEN YOU GET UP. BIND THEM AS A SIGN ON YOUR HAND AND LET THEM BE A SYMBOL ON YOUR FOREHEAD. WRITE THEM ON THE DOORPOSTS OF YOUR HOUSE AND ON YOUR GATES.

5 Minute Journaling

WHAT AM I BATTLING TO PUT GOD FIRST?

WHERE AM I BATTLING TO TRUST GOD AND HAVE FAITH?

HOW AM I BATTLING TO WORSHIP GOD ALONE?

Prayer & Meditation

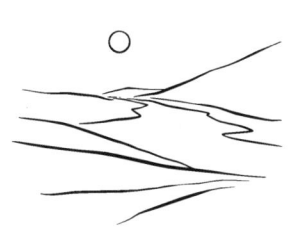

PRAY FOR GOD TO HELP YOU WIN THESE BATTLES.

_____
_____
_____
_____
_____
_____
_____
_____

READ, WRITE, SAY, SING, AND MOVE TO THIS DAY'S VERSE

_____
_____
_____
_____
_____
_____
_____

5 Minute Journaling

WHAT AM I BATTLING TO PUT GOD FIRST?

WHERE AM I BATTLING TO TRUST GOD AND HAVE FAITH?

HOW AM I BATTLING TO WORSHIP GOD ALONE?

Prayer & Meditation

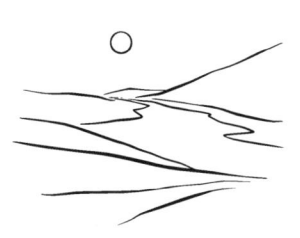

PRAY FOR GOD TO HELP YOU WIN THESE BATTLES.

_____
_____
_____
_____
_____
_____
_____
_____

READ, WRITE, SAY, SING, AND MOVE TO THIS DAY'S VERSE

_____
_____
_____
_____
_____
_____
_____

5 Minute Journaling

WHAT AM I BATTLING TO PUT GOD FIRST?

WHERE AM I BATTLING TO TRUST GOD AND HAVE FAITH?

HOW AM I BATTLING TO WORSHIP GOD ALONE?

Prayer & Meditation

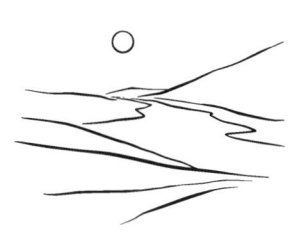

PRAY FOR GOD TO HELP YOU WIN THESE BATTLES.

_____
_____
_____
_____
_____
_____
_____
_____

READ, WRITE, SAY, SING, AND MOVE TO THIS DAY'S VERSE

_____
_____
_____
_____
_____
_____
_____
_____

5 Minute Journaling

WHAT AM I BATTLING TO PUT GOD FIRST?

WHERE AM I BATTLING TO TRUST GOD AND HAVE FAITH?

HOW AM I BATTLING TO WORSHIP GOD ALONE?

Prayer & Meditation

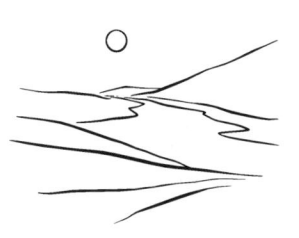

PRAY FOR GOD TO HELP YOU WIN THESE BATTLES.

_____
_____
_____
_____
_____
_____
_____
_____

READ, WRITE, SAY, SING, AND MOVE TO THIS DAY'S VERSE

_____
_____
_____
_____
_____
_____
_____

5 Minute Journaling

WHAT AM I BATTLING TO PUT GOD FIRST?

_____
_____
_____
_____
_____

WHERE AM I BATTLING TO TRUST GOD AND HAVE FAITH?

_____
_____
_____
_____
_____

HOW AM I BATTLING TO WORSHIP GOD ALONE?

_____
_____
_____
_____
_____

Prayer & Meditation

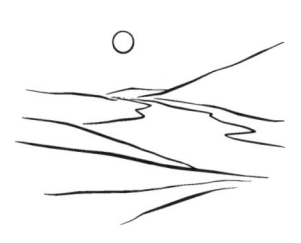

PRAY FOR GOD TO HELP YOU WIN THESE BATTLES.

_____

_____

_____

_____

_____

_____

_____

READ, WRITE, SAY, SING, AND MOVE TO THIS DAY'S VERSE

_____

_____

_____

_____

_____

_____

_____

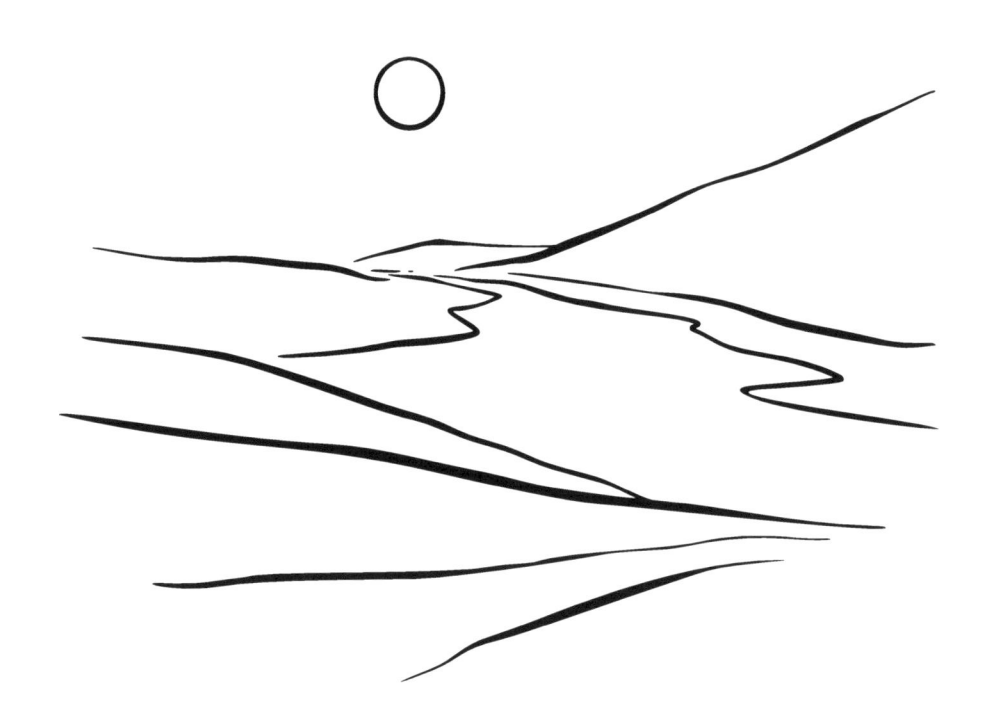

Verse Four

DEUTERONOMY 8:17-18

YOU MAY SAY TO YOURSELF, 'MY POWER AND MY OWN ABILITY HAVE GAINED THIS WEALTH FOR ME,' BUT REMEMBER THAT THE LORD YOUR GOD GIVES YOU THE POWER TO GAIN WEALTH, IN ORDER TO CONFIRM HIS COVENANT HE SWORE TO YOUR FATHERS, AS IT IS TODAY.

5 Minute Journaling

WHAT AM I BATTLING TO PUT GOD FIRST?

_____
_____
_____
_____
_____

WHERE AM I BATTLING TO TRUST GOD AND HAVE FAITH?

_____
_____
_____
_____
_____

HOW AM I BATTLING TO WORSHIP GOD ALONE?

_____
_____
_____
_____
_____

Prayer & Meditation

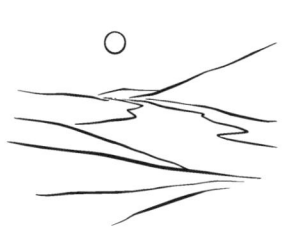

PRAY FOR GOD TO HELP YOU WIN THESE BATTLES.

_____
_____
_____
_____
_____
_____
_____
_____

READ, WRITE, SAY, SING, AND MOVE TO THIS DAY'S VERSE

_____
_____
_____
_____
_____
_____
_____

5 Minute Journaling

WHAT AM I BATTLING TO PUT GOD FIRST?

_____
_____
_____
_____
_____

WHERE AM I BATTLING TO TRUST GOD AND HAVE FAITH?

_____
_____
_____
_____
_____

HOW AM I BATTLING TO WORSHIP GOD ALONE?

_____
_____
_____
_____
_____

Prayer & Meditation

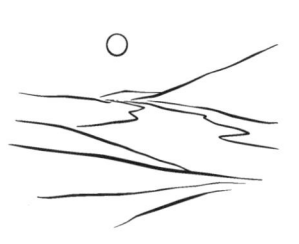

PRAY FOR GOD TO HELP YOU WIN THESE BATTLES.

_____
_____
_____
_____
_____
_____
_____
_____

READ, WRITE, SAY, SING, AND MOVE TO THIS DAY'S VERSE

_____
_____
_____
_____
_____
_____
_____

5 Minute Journaling

WHAT AM I BATTLING TO PUT GOD FIRST?

___

___

___

___

WHERE AM I BATTLING TO TRUST GOD AND HAVE FAITH?

___

___

___

___

HOW AM I BATTLING TO WORSHIP GOD ALONE?

___

___

___

___

Prayer & Meditation

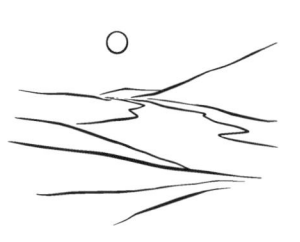

PRAY FOR GOD TO HELP YOU WIN THESE BATTLES.

_____
_____
_____
_____
_____
_____
_____
_____
_____

READ, WRITE, SAY, SING, AND MOVE TO THIS DAY'S VERSE

_____
_____
_____
_____
_____
_____
_____

5 Minute Journaling

WHAT AM I BATTLING TO PUT GOD FIRST?

_____
_____
_____
_____
_____

WHERE AM I BATTLING TO TRUST GOD AND HAVE FAITH?

_____
_____
_____
_____
_____

HOW AM I BATTLING TO WORSHIP GOD ALONE?

_____
_____
_____
_____
_____

Prayer & Meditation

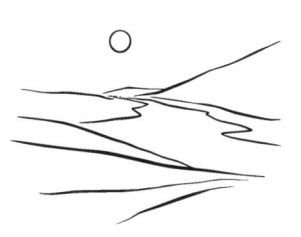

PRAY FOR GOD TO HELP YOU WIN THESE BATTLES.

_____
_____
_____
_____
_____
_____
_____
_____

READ, WRITE, SAY, SING, AND MOVE TO THIS DAY'S VERSE

_____
_____
_____
_____
_____
_____
_____

5 Minute Journaling

WHAT AM I BATTLING TO PUT GOD FIRST?

WHERE AM I BATTLING TO TRUST GOD AND HAVE FAITH?

HOW AM I BATTLING TO WORSHIP GOD ALONE?

Prayer & Meditation

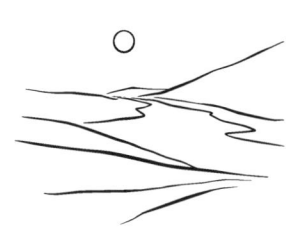

PRAY FOR GOD TO HELP YOU WIN THESE BATTLES.

_____
_____
_____
_____
_____
_____
_____
_____

READ, WRITE, SAY, SING, AND MOVE TO THIS DAY'S VERSE

_____
_____
_____
_____
_____
_____
_____

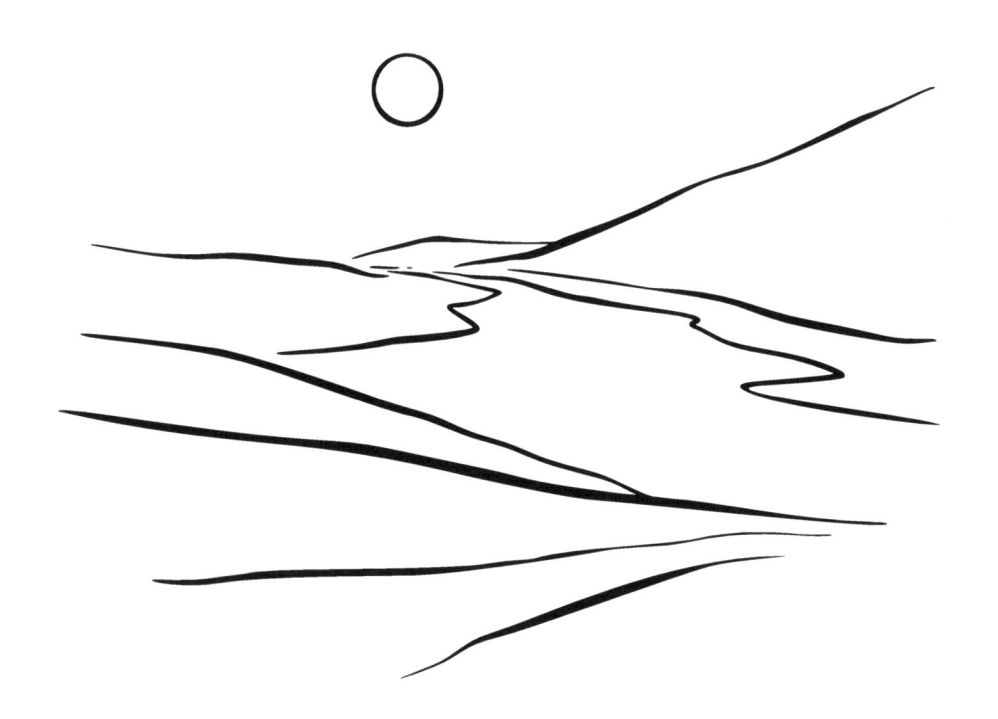

Verse Five

DEUTERONOMY 10:12

ISRAEL, WHAT DOES THE LORD YOUR GOD ASK OF YOU EXCEPT TO FEAR THE LORD YOUR GOD BY WALKING IN ALL HIS WAYS, TO LOVE HIM, AND TO WORSHIP THE LORD YOUR GOD WITH ALL YOUR HEART AND ALL YOUR SOUL?

5 Minute Journaling

WHAT AM I BATTLING TO PUT GOD FIRST?

_____
_____
_____
_____
_____

WHERE AM I BATTLING TO TRUST GOD AND HAVE FAITH?

_____
_____
_____
_____
_____

HOW AM I BATTLING TO WORSHIP GOD ALONE?

_____
_____
_____
_____
_____

Prayer & Meditation

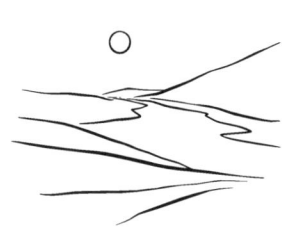

PRAY FOR GOD TO HELP YOU WIN THESE BATTLES.

_____
_____
_____
_____
_____
_____
_____
_____
_____

READ, WRITE, SAY, SING, AND MOVE TO THIS DAY'S VERSE

_____
_____
_____
_____
_____
_____
_____
_____

5 Minute Journaling

WHAT AM I BATTLING TO PUT GOD FIRST?

WHERE AM I BATTLING TO TRUST GOD AND HAVE FAITH?

HOW AM I BATTLING TO WORSHIP GOD ALONE?

Prayer & Meditation

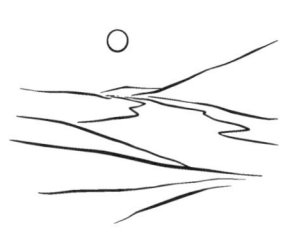

PRAY FOR GOD TO HELP YOU WIN THESE BATTLES.

_____
_____
_____
_____
_____
_____
_____
_____

READ, WRITE, SAY, SING, AND MOVE TO THIS DAY'S VERSE

_____
_____
_____
_____
_____
_____

5 Minute Journaling

WHAT AM I BATTLING TO PUT GOD FIRST?

_____
_____
_____
_____
_____
_____

WHERE AM I BATTLING TO TRUST GOD AND HAVE FAITH?

_____
_____
_____
_____
_____
_____

HOW AM I BATTLING TO WORSHIP GOD ALONE?

_____
_____
_____
_____
_____
_____

Prayer & Meditation

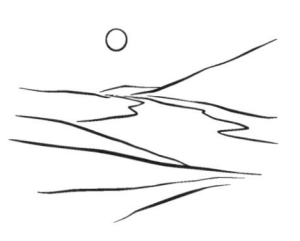

PRAY FOR GOD TO HELP YOU WIN THESE BATTLES.

_____
_____
_____
_____
_____
_____
_____
_____

READ, WRITE, SAY, SING, AND MOVE TO THIS DAY'S VERSE

_____
_____
_____
_____
_____
_____

5 Minute Journaling

WHAT AM I BATTLING TO PUT GOD FIRST?

_____
_____
_____
_____
_____

WHERE AM I BATTLING TO TRUST GOD AND HAVE FAITH?

_____
_____
_____
_____
_____

HOW AM I BATTLING TO WORSHIP GOD ALONE?

_____
_____
_____
_____
_____

Prayer & Meditation

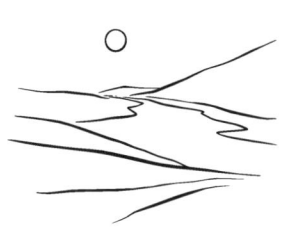

PRAY FOR GOD TO HELP YOU WIN THESE BATTLES.

_____
_____
_____
_____
_____
_____
_____
_____

READ, WRITE, SAY, SING, AND MOVE TO THIS DAY'S VERSE

_____
_____
_____
_____
_____
_____
_____
_____

5 Minute Journaling

WHAT AM I BATTLING TO PUT GOD FIRST?

_____
_____
_____
_____
_____

WHERE AM I BATTLING TO TRUST GOD AND HAVE FAITH?

_____
_____
_____
_____
_____

HOW AM I BATTLING TO WORSHIP GOD ALONE?

_____
_____
_____
_____
_____

Prayer & Meditation

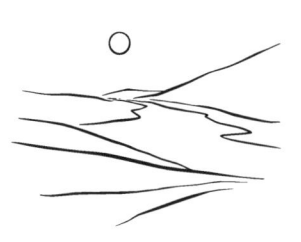

PRAY FOR GOD TO HELP YOU WIN THESE BATTLES.

_____
_____
_____
_____
_____
_____
_____
_____
_____
_____

READ, WRITE, SAY, SING, AND MOVE TO THIS DAY'S VERSE

_____
_____
_____
_____
_____
_____
_____
_____

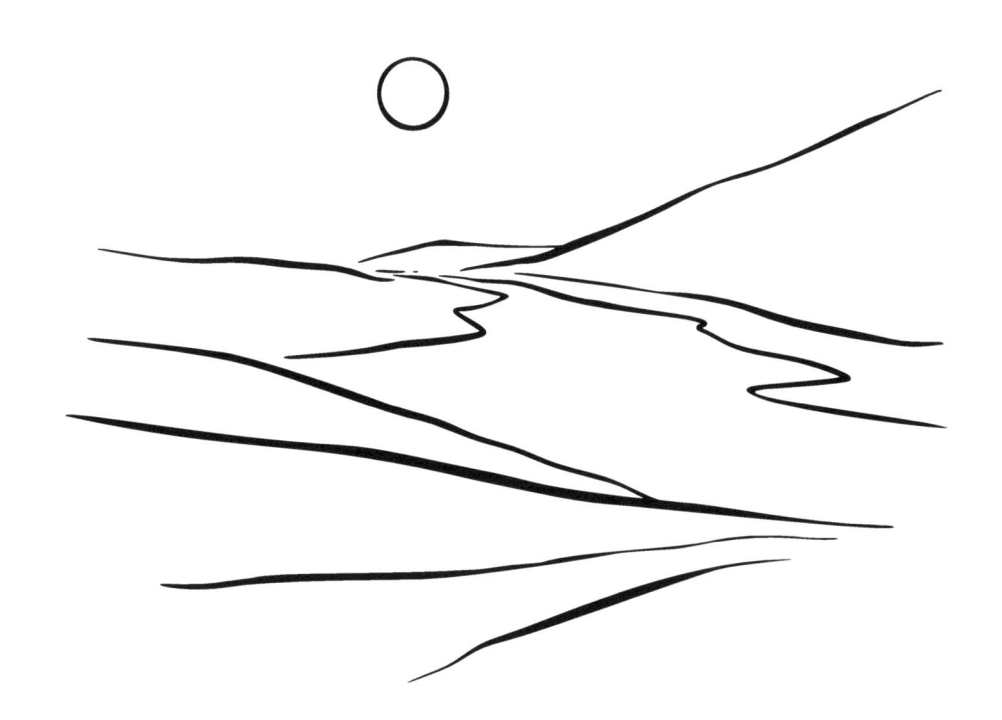

Verse Six

DEUTERONOMY 29:29

THE HIDDEN THINGS BELONG TO THE LORD OUR GOD, BUT THE REVEALED THINGS BELONG TO US AND OUR CHILDREN FOREVER, SO THAT WE MAY FOLLOW ALL THE WORDS OF THIS LAW.

5 Minute Journaling

WHAT AM I BATTLING TO PUT GOD FIRST?

___

___

___

___

___

WHERE AM I BATTLING TO TRUST GOD AND HAVE FAITH?

___

___

___

___

___

HOW AM I BATTLING TO WORSHIP GOD ALONE?

___

___

___

___

___

Prayer & Meditation

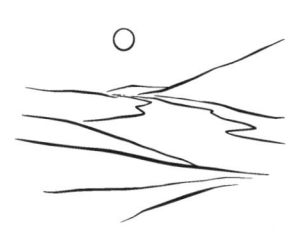

PRAY FOR GOD TO HELP YOU WIN THESE BATTLES.

_____

READ, WRITE, SAY, SING, AND MOVE TO THIS DAY'S VERSE

_____

5 Minute Journaling

WHAT AM I BATTLING TO PUT GOD FIRST?

_____
_____
_____
_____
_____

WHERE AM I BATTLING TO TRUST GOD AND HAVE FAITH?

_____
_____
_____
_____
_____

HOW AM I BATTLING TO WORSHIP GOD ALONE?

_____
_____
_____
_____
_____

Prayer & Meditation

PRAY FOR GOD TO HELP YOU WIN THESE BATTLES.

READ, WRITE, SAY, SING, AND MOVE TO THIS DAY'S VERSE

5 Minute Journaling

WHAT AM I BATTLING TO PUT GOD FIRST?

_____
_____
_____
_____
_____

WHERE AM I BATTLING TO TRUST GOD AND HAVE FAITH?

_____
_____
_____
_____
_____

HOW AM I BATTLING TO WORSHIP GOD ALONE?

_____
_____
_____
_____
_____

Prayer & Meditation

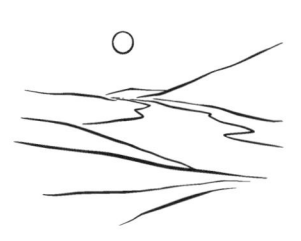

PRAY FOR GOD TO HELP YOU WIN THESE BATTLES.

_____
_____
_____
_____
_____
_____
_____
_____

READ, WRITE, SAY, SING, AND MOVE TO THIS DAY'S VERSE

_____
_____
_____
_____
_____
_____
_____

5 Minute Journaling

WHAT AM I BATTLING TO PUT GOD FIRST?

_____
_____
_____
_____
_____

WHERE AM I BATTLING TO TRUST GOD AND HAVE FAITH?

_____
_____
_____
_____
_____

HOW AM I BATTLING TO WORSHIP GOD ALONE?

_____
_____
_____
_____
_____

Prayer & Meditation

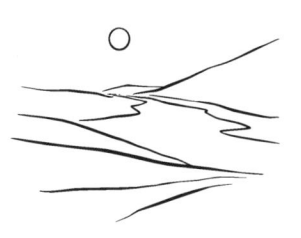

PRAY FOR GOD TO HELP YOU WIN THESE BATTLES.

_____
_____
_____
_____
_____
_____
_____
_____
_____

READ, WRITE, SAY, SING, AND MOVE TO THIS DAY'S VERSE

_____
_____
_____
_____
_____
_____
_____

5 Minute Journaling

WHAT AM I BATTLING TO PUT GOD FIRST?

_____
_____
_____
_____
_____

WHERE AM I BATTLING TO TRUST GOD AND HAVE FAITH?

_____
_____
_____
_____
_____

HOW AM I BATTLING TO WORSHIP GOD ALONE?

_____
_____
_____
_____
_____

Prayer & Meditation

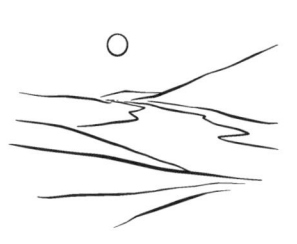

PRAY FOR GOD TO HELP YOU WIN THESE BATTLES.

_____
_____
_____
_____
_____
_____
_____
_____

READ, WRITE, SAY, SING, AND MOVE TO THIS DAY'S VERSE

_____
_____
_____
_____
_____
_____
_____

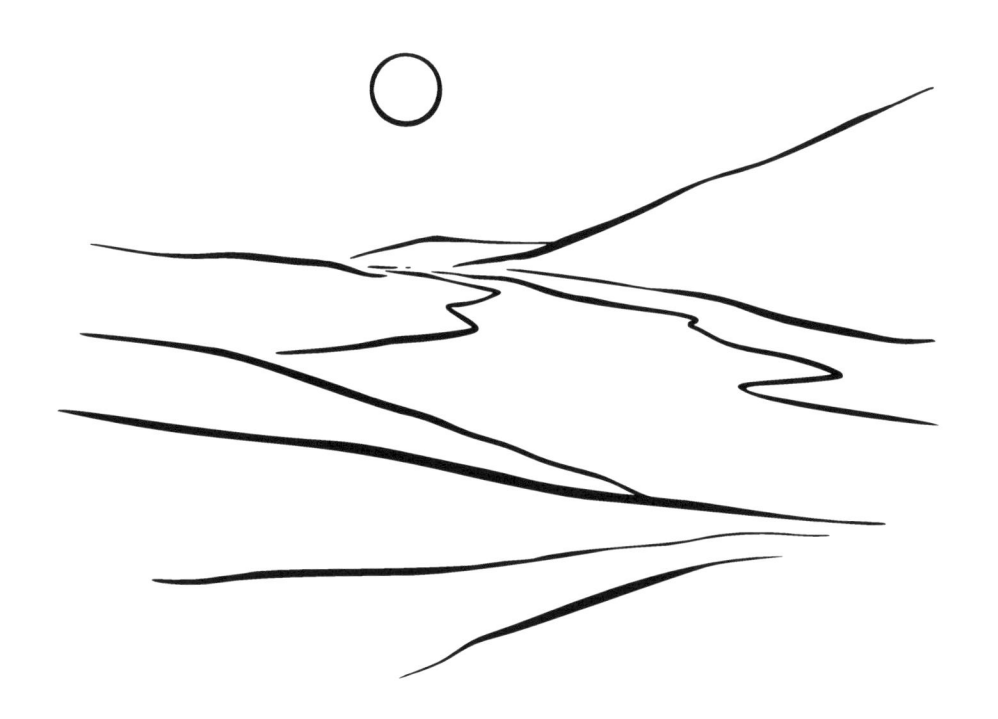

Verse Seven

DEUTERONOMY 30:15-16

TODAY I HAVE SET BEFORE YOU LIFE AND PROSPERITY, DEATH AND ADVERSITY. FOR I AM COMMANDING YOU TODAY TO LOVE THE LORD YOUR GOD, TO WALK IN HIS WAYS, AND TO KEEP HIS COMMANDS, STATUTES, AND ORDINANCES, SO THAT YOU MAY LIVE AND MULTIPLY, AND THE LORD YOUR GOD MAY BLESS YOU IN THE LAND YOU ARE ENTERING TO POSSESS.

5 Minute Journaling

WHAT AM I BATTLING TO PUT GOD FIRST?

WHERE AM I BATTLING TO TRUST GOD AND HAVE FAITH?

HOW AM I BATTLING TO WORSHIP GOD ALONE?

Prayer & Meditation

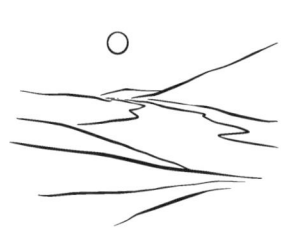

PRAY FOR GOD TO HELP YOU WIN THESE BATTLES.

_____
_____
_____
_____
_____
_____
_____
_____

READ, WRITE, SAY, SING, AND MOVE TO THIS DAY'S VERSE

_____
_____
_____
_____
_____
_____

5 Minute Journaling

WHAT AM I BATTLING TO PUT GOD FIRST?

_____
_____
_____
_____

WHERE AM I BATTLING TO TRUST GOD AND HAVE FAITH?

_____
_____
_____
_____

HOW AM I BATTLING TO WORSHIP GOD ALONE?

_____
_____
_____
_____

Prayer & Meditation

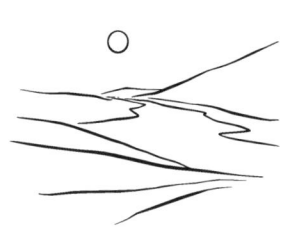

PRAY FOR GOD TO HELP YOU WIN THESE BATTLES.

_____
_____
_____
_____
_____
_____
_____
_____

READ, WRITE, SAY, SING, AND MOVE TO THIS DAY'S VERSE

_____
_____
_____
_____
_____
_____

5 Minute Journaling

WHAT AM I BATTLING TO PUT GOD FIRST?

_____
_____
_____
_____
_____

WHERE AM I BATTLING TO TRUST GOD AND HAVE FAITH?

_____
_____
_____
_____
_____

HOW AM I BATTLING TO WORSHIP GOD ALONE?

_____
_____
_____
_____
_____

Prayer & Meditation

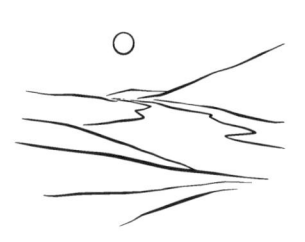

PRAY FOR GOD TO HELP YOU WIN THESE BATTLES.

_____
_____
_____
_____
_____
_____
_____
_____

READ, WRITE, SAY, SING, AND MOVE TO THIS DAY'S VERSE

_____
_____
_____
_____
_____
_____
_____

5 Minute Journaling

WHAT AM I BATTLING TO PUT GOD FIRST?

_____
_____
_____
_____
_____

WHERE AM I BATTLING TO TRUST GOD AND HAVE FAITH?

_____
_____
_____
_____
_____

HOW AM I BATTLING TO WORSHIP GOD ALONE?

_____
_____
_____
_____
_____

Prayer & Meditation

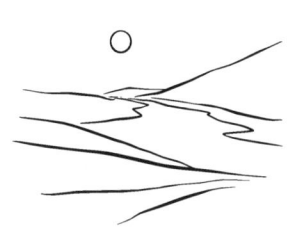

PRAY FOR GOD TO HELP YOU WIN THESE BATTLES.

READ, WRITE, SAY, SING, AND MOVE TO THIS DAY'S VERSE

5 Minute Journaling

WHAT AM I BATTLING TO PUT GOD FIRST?

WHERE AM I BATTLING TO TRUST GOD AND HAVE FAITH?

HOW AM I BATTLING TO WORSHIP GOD ALONE?

Prayer & Meditation

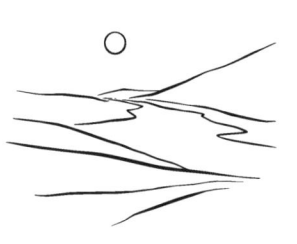

PRAY FOR GOD TO HELP YOU WIN THESE BATTLES.

_____
_____
_____
_____
_____
_____
_____
_____

READ, WRITE, SAY, SING, AND MOVE TO THIS DAY'S VERSE

_____
_____
_____
_____
_____
_____
_____

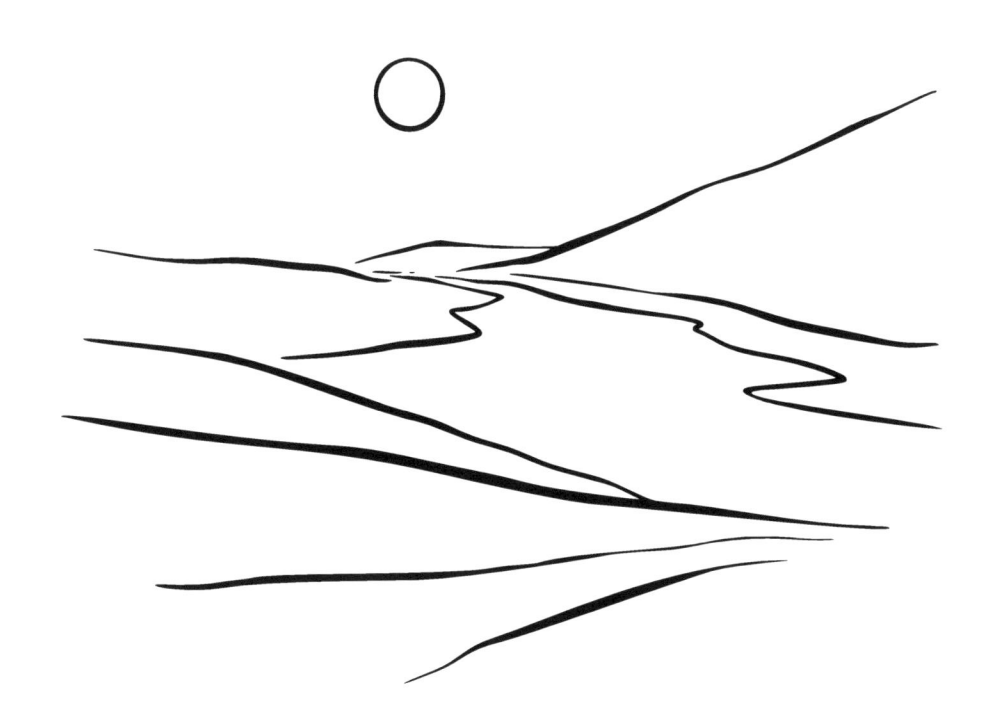

Verse Eight

DEUTERONOMY 32:3-4

FOR I WILL PROCLAIM YAHWEH'S NAME. DECLARE THE GREATNESS OF OUR GOD!
THE ROCK—HIS WORK IS PERFECT;
ALL HIS WAYS ARE ENTIRELY JUST.
A FAITHFUL GOD, WITHOUT PREJUDICE,
HE IS RIGHTEOUS AND TRUE.

5 Minute Journaling

WHAT AM I BATTLING TO PUT GOD FIRST?

_____
_____
_____
_____
_____

WHERE AM I BATTLING TO TRUST GOD AND HAVE FAITH?

_____
_____
_____
_____
_____

HOW AM I BATTLING TO WORSHIP GOD ALONE?

_____
_____
_____
_____
_____

Prayer & Meditation

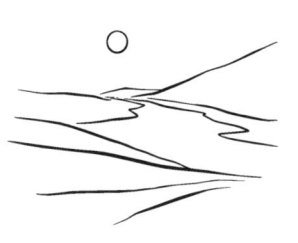

PRAY FOR GOD TO HELP YOU WIN THESE BATTLES.

_____
_____
_____
_____
_____
_____
_____
_____

READ, WRITE, SAY, SING, AND MOVE TO THIS DAY'S VERSE

_____
_____
_____
_____
_____
_____
_____

5 Minute Journaling

WHAT AM I BATTLING TO PUT GOD FIRST?

_____
_____
_____
_____
_____

WHERE AM I BATTLING TO TRUST GOD AND HAVE FAITH?

_____
_____
_____
_____
_____

HOW AM I BATTLING TO WORSHIP GOD ALONE?

_____
_____
_____
_____
_____

Prayer & Meditation

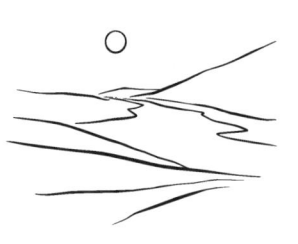

PRAY FOR GOD TO HELP YOU WIN THESE BATTLES.

_____
_____
_____
_____
_____
_____
_____
_____
_____

READ, WRITE, SAY, SING, AND MOVE TO THIS DAY'S VERSE

_____
_____
_____
_____
_____
_____
_____
_____

5 Minute Journaling

WHAT AM I BATTLING TO PUT GOD FIRST?

_____
_____
_____
_____
_____

WHERE AM I BATTLING TO TRUST GOD AND HAVE FAITH?

_____
_____
_____
_____
_____

HOW AM I BATTLING TO WORSHIP GOD ALONE?

_____
_____
_____
_____
_____

Prayer & Meditation

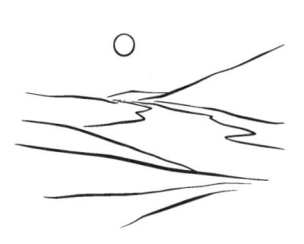

PRAY FOR GOD TO HELP YOU WIN THESE BATTLES.

_____
_____
_____
_____
_____
_____
_____
_____

READ, WRITE, SAY, SING, AND MOVE TO THIS DAY'S VERSE

_____
_____
_____
_____
_____
_____

5 Minute Journaling

WHAT AM I BATTLING TO PUT GOD FIRST?

_____

_____

_____

_____

_____

WHERE AM I BATTLING TO TRUST GOD AND HAVE FAITH?

_____

_____

_____

_____

_____

HOW AM I BATTLING TO WORSHIP GOD ALONE?

_____

_____

_____

_____

_____

Prayer & Meditation

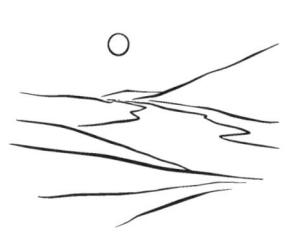

PRAY FOR GOD TO HELP YOU WIN THESE BATTLES.

_____
_____
_____
_____
_____
_____
_____
_____

READ, WRITE, SAY, SING, AND MOVE TO THIS DAY'S VERSE

_____
_____
_____
_____
_____
_____
_____

5 Minute Journaling

WHAT AM I BATTLING TO PUT GOD FIRST?

_____
_____
_____
_____
_____

WHERE AM I BATTLING TO TRUST GOD AND HAVE FAITH?

_____
_____
_____
_____
_____

HOW AM I BATTLING TO WORSHIP GOD ALONE?

_____
_____
_____
_____
_____

Prayer & Meditation

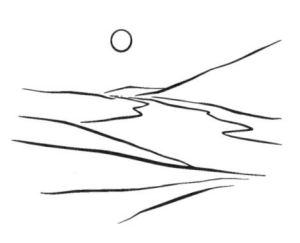

PRAY FOR GOD TO HELP YOU WIN THESE BATTLES.

_____
_____
_____
_____
_____
_____
_____
_____

READ, WRITE, SAY, SING, AND MOVE TO THIS DAY'S VERSE

_____
_____
_____
_____
_____
_____
_____

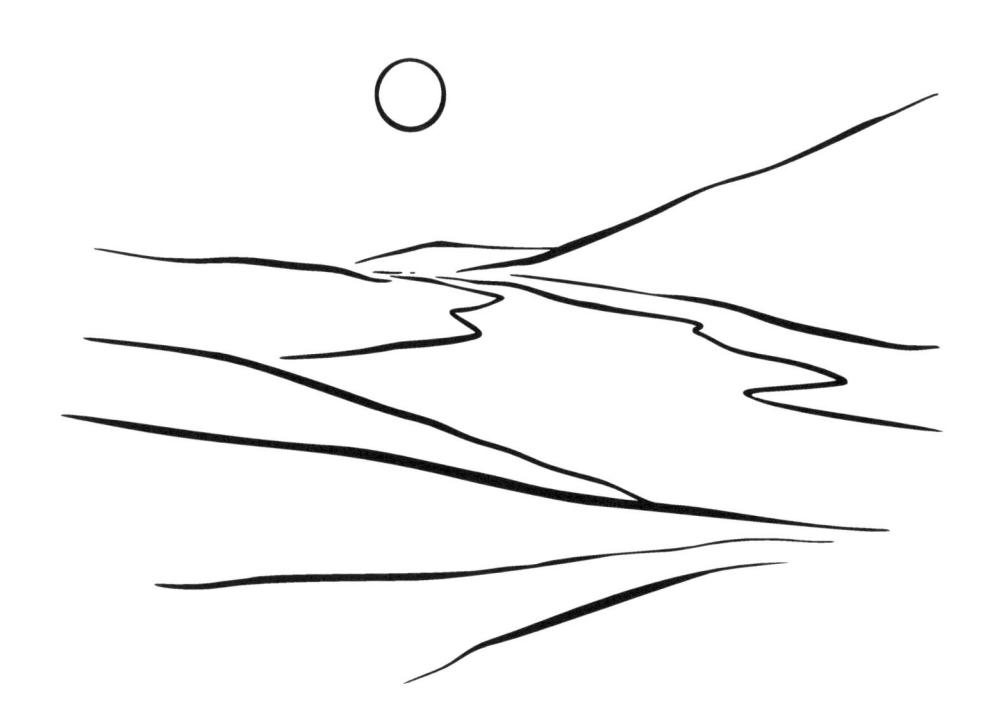

Made in the USA
Columbia, SC
13 February 2023